This Budget Planner
belongs to:

_____

My Plan to
Get Rich Quick :
Earn
Save
Grow Rich !

Savings Tracker

Date	Transaction	Deposited	Withdrawn	Balance
	Starting Balance			

Savings Tracker

Date	Transaction	Deposited	Withdrawn	Balance

Debt Tracker

Date	Deposited	Balance
	Starting balance	

Debt Tracker

Date	Deposited	Balance

Monthly Budget

Income

Income 1	
Income 2	
Other Income	
Total Income	

Expenses

Month

Budget

Bill to be paid	Date due	Amount	Paid	Notes

Other Expenses

other Expenses	Date	Amount	Paid	Notes
Total				

Notes:

Total Income

Total Expenses

Difference

Weekly Expense Tracker

Monday Date ___ / ___ / ___

Description	Amount
Total	

Tuesday Date ___ / ___ / ___

Description	Amount
Total	

Wednesday Date ___ / ___ / ___

Description	Amount
Total	

Thursday Date ___ / ___ / ___

Description	Amount
Total	

Budget: _____

Brought forward: _____

Weekly Expense Tracker

Friday Date ___ /___ /___

Description	Amount
Total	

Saturday Date ___ /___ /___

Description	Amount
Total	

Sunday Date ___ /___ /___

Description	Amount
Total	

Notes

Budget:

Brought forward:

Weekly Expense Tracker

Monday Date ___ /___ /___

Description	Amount
Total	

Tuesday Date ___ /___ /___

Description	Amount
Total	

Wednesday Date ___ /___ /___

Description	Amount
Total	

Thursday Date ___ /___ /___

Description	Amount
Total	

Budget:

Brought Forward:

Weekly Expense Tracker

Friday   Date ___ /___ /___

Description	Amount
Total	

Saturday   Date ___ /___ /___

Description	Amount
Total	

Sunday Date ___ /___ /___

Description	Amount
Total	

Notes

Budget:

Brought forward:

Weekly Expense Tracker

Monday
Date ___ /___ /___

Description	Amount
Total	

Tuesday
Date ___ /___ /___

Description	Amount
Total	

Wednesday
Date ___ /___ /___

Description	Amount
Total	

Thursday
Date ___ /___ /___

Description	Amount
Total	

Budget:

Brought forward:

Weekly Expense Tracker

Friday Date ___ /___ /___

Description	Amount
Total	

Saturday Date ___ /___ /___

Description	Amount
Total	

Sunday Date ___ /___ /___

Description	Amount
Total	

Notes

Budget:

Brought forward:

Weekly Expense Tracker

Monday   Date ___ /___ /___

Description	Amount
Total	

Tuesday   Date ___ /___ /___

Description	Amount
Total	

Wednesday   Date ___ /___ /___

Description	Amount
Total	

Thursday   Date ___ /___ /___

Description	Amount
Total	

Budget: _____   Brought Forward: _____

Weekly Expense Tracker

Friday
Date ___ /___ /___

Description	Amount
Total	

Saturday
Date ___ /___ /___

Description	Amount
Total	

Sunday
Date ___ /___ /___

Description	Amount
Total	

Notes

Budget:

Brought forward:

Weekly Expense Tracker

Monday   Date ___ /___ /___

Description	Amount
Total	

Tuesday   Date ___ /___ /___

Description	Amount
Total	

Wednesday   Date ___ /___ /___

Description	Amount
Total	

Thursday   Date ___ /___ /___

Description	Amount
Total	

Budget:

Brought forward:

Weekly Expense Tracker

Friday Date ___ /___ /___

Description	Amount
Total	

Saturday Date ___ /___ /___

Description	Amount
Total	

Sunday Date ___ /___ /___

Description	Amount
Total	

Notes

Budget:

Brought forward:

Monthly Budget

Income

Expenses

Income 1	
Income 2	
Other Income	
Total Income	

Month

Budget

Bill to be paid	Date due	Amount	Paid	Notes

Other Expenses

Other Expenses	Date	Amount	Paid	Notes
Total				

Notes:

Total Income

Total Expenses

Difference

Weekly Expense Tracker

Monday   Date ___ /___ /___

Description	Amount
Total	

Tuesday   Date ___ /___ /___

Description	Amount
Total	

Wednesday   Date ___ /___ /___

Description	Amount
Total	

Thursday   Date ___ /___ /___

Description	Amount
Total	

Budget:

Brought forward:

Weekly Expense Tracker

Friday   Date ___ /___ /___

Description	Amount
Total	

Saturday   Date ___ /___ /___

Description	Amount
Total	

Sunday   Date ___ /___ /___

Description	Amount
Total	

Notes

Budget:

Brought forward:

Weekly Expense Tracker

Monday   Date ___ /___ /___

Description	Amount
Total	

Tuesday   Date ___ /___ /___

Description	Amount
Total	

Wednesday Date ___ /___ /___

Description	Amount
Total	

Thursday Date ___ /___ /___

Description	Amount
Total	

Budget:

Brought forward:

Weekly Expense Tracker

Friday
Date ___ /___ /___

Description	Amount
Total	

Saturday
Date ___ /___ /___

Description	Amount
Total	

Sunday
Date ___ /___ /___

Description	Amount
Total	

Notes

Budget:

Brought Forward:

Weekly Expense Tracker

Monday
Date ___ /___ /___

Description	Amount
Total	

Tuesday
Date ___ /___ /___

Description	Amount
Total	

Wednesday
Date ___ /___ /___

Description	Amount
Total	

Thursday
Date ___ /___ /___

Description	Amount
Total	

Budget:

Brought forward:

Weekly Expense Tracker

Friday
Date ___ /___ /___

Description	Amount
Total	

Saturday
Date ___ /___ /___

Description	Amount
Total	

Sunday
Date ___ /___ /___

Description	Amount
Total	

Notes

Budget:

Brought Forward:

Weekly Expense Tracker

Monday
Date ___ /___ /___

Description	Amount
Total	

Tuesday
Date ___ /___ /___

Description	Amount
Total	

Wednesday
Date ___ /___ /___

Description	Amount
Total	

Thursday
Date ___ /___ /___

Description	Amount
Total	

Budget:

Brought Forward:

Weekly Expense Tracker

Friday   Date ___ /___ /___

Description	Amount
Total	

Saturday   Date ___ /___ /___

Description	Amount
Total	

Sunday   Date ___ /___ /___

Description	Amount
Total	

Notes

Budget: ___

Brought forward: ___

Weekly Expense Tracker

Monday Date ___ /___ /___

Description	Amount
Total	

Tuesday Date ___ /___ /___

Description	Amount
Total	

Wednesday Date ___ /___ /___

Description	Amount
Total	

Thursday Date ___ /___ /___

Description	Amount
Total	

Budget:

Brought forward:

Weekly Expense Tracker

Friday Date ___ /___ /___

Description	Amount
Total	

Saturday Date ___ /___ /___

Description	Amount
Total	

Sunday Date ___ /___ /___

Description	Amount
Total	

Notes

Budget:

Brought forward:

Monthly Budget

Income

Income 1	
Income 2	
Other Income	
Total Income	

Expenses

Month

Budget

Bill to be paid	Date due	Amount	Paid	Notes

Other Expenses

Other Expenses	Date	Amount	Paid	Notes
Total				

Total Income

Total Expenses

Difference

Notes:

_____

_____

_____

_____

_____

Weekly Expense Tracker

Monday   Date ___ /___ /___

Description	Amount
Total	

Tuesday   Date ___ /___ /___

Description	Amount
Total	

Wednesday   Date ___ /___ /___

Description	Amount
Total	

Thursday   Date ___ /___ /___

Description	Amount
Total	

Budget: _____

Brought forward: _____

Weekly Expense Tracker

Friday   Date ___ /___ /___

Description	Amount
Total	

Saturday   Date ___ /___ /___

Description	Amount
Total	

Sunday   Date ___ /___ /___

Description	Amount
Total	

Notes

Budget:

Brought forward:

Weekly Expense Tracker

Monday
Date ___ / ___ / ___

Description	Amount
Total	

Tuesday
Date ___ / ___ / ___

Description	Amount
Total	

Wednesday
Date ___ / ___ / ___

Description	Amount
Total	

Thursday
Date ___ / ___ / ___

Description	Amount
Total	

Budget:

Brought forward:

Weekly Expense Tracker

Friday
Date ___ /___ /___

Description	Amount
Total	

Saturday
Date ___ /___ /___

Description	Amount
Total	

Sunday
Date ___ /___ /___

Description	Amount
Total	

Notes

Budget:

Brought forward:

Weekly Expense Tracker

Monday Date ___ /___ /___

Description	Amount
Total	

Tuesday Date ___ /___ /___

Description	Amount
Total	

Wednesday Date ___ /___ /___

Description	Amount
Total	

Thursday Date ___ /___ /___

Description	Amount
Total	

Budget:

Brought forward:

Weekly Expense Tracker

Friday
Date ___ /___ /___

Description	Amount
Total	

Saturday
Date ___ /___ /___

Description	Amount
Total	

Sunday
Date ___ /___ /___

Description	Amount
Total	

Notes

Budget:

Brought forward:

Weekly Expense Tracker

Monday   Date ___ /___ /___

Description	Amount
Total	

Tuesday   Date ___ /___ /___

Description	Amount
Total	

Wednesday   Date ___ /___ /___

Description	Amount
Total	

Thursday   Date ___ /___ /___

Description	Amount
Total	

Budget:

Brought forward:

Weekly Expense Tracker

Friday
Date ___ /___ /___

Description	Amount
Total	

Saturday
Date ___ /___ /___

Description	Amount
Total	

Sunday
Date ___ /___ /___

Description	Amount
Total	

Notes

Budget:

Brought forward:

Weekly Expense Tracker

Monday Date ___ /___ /___

Description	Amount
Total	

Tuesday Date ___ /___ /___

Description	Amount
Total	

Wednesday Date ___ /___ /___

Description	Amount
Total	

Thursday Date ___ /___ /___

Description	Amount
Total	

Budget: _____

Brought forward: _____

Weekly Expense Tracker

Friday   Date ___ /___ /___

Description	Amount
Total	

Saturday   Date ___ /___ /___

Description	Amount
Total	

Sunday   Date ___ /___ /___

Description	Amount
Total	

Notes

Budget:

Brought Forward:

Monthly Budget

Income

Income 1	
Income 2	
Other Income	
Total Income	

Expenses

Month

Budget

Bill to be paid	Date due	Amount	Paid	Notes

Other Expenses

Other Expenses	Date	Amount	Paid	Notes
Total				

Total Income

Total Expenses

Difference

Notes:

Weekly Expense Tracker

Monday   Date ___ /___ /___

Description	Amount
Total	

Tuesday   Date ___ /___ /___

Description	Amount
Total	

Wednesday   Date ___ /___ /___

Description	Amount
Total	

Thursday   Date ___ /___ /___

Description	Amount
Total	

Budget:

Brought forward:

Weekly Expense Tracker

Friday   Date ___ /___ /___

Description	Amount
Total	

Saturday   Date ___ /___ /___

Description	Amount
Total	

Sunday   Date ___ /___ /___

Description	Amount
Total	

Notes

Budget:

Brought Forward:

Weekly Expense Tracker

Monday Date ___ /___ /___

Description	Amount
Total	

Tuesday Date ___ /___ /___

Description	Amount
Total	

Wednesday Date ___ /___ /___

Description	Amount
Total	

Thursday Date ___ /___ /___

Description	Amount
Total	

Budget:

Brought Forward:

Weekly Expense Tracker

Friday   Date ___ /___ /___

Description	Amount
Total	

Saturday   Date ___ /___ /___

Description	Amount
Total	

Sunday Date ___ /___ /___

Description	Amount
Total	

Notes

Budget: Brought forward:

Weekly Expense Tracker

Monday
Date ___ /___ /___

Description	Amount
Total	

Tuesday
Date ___ /___ /___

Description	Amount
Total	

Wednesday
Date ___ /___ /___

Description	Amount
Total	

Thursday
Date ___ /___ /___

Description	Amount
Total	

Budget:

Brought forward:

Weekly Expense Tracker

Friday   Date ___ /___ /___

Description	Amount
Total	

Saturday   Date ___ /___ /___

Description	Amount
Total	

Sunday   Date ___ /___ /___

Description	Amount
Total	

Notes

Budget:

Brought forward:

Weekly Expense Tracker

Monday   Date ___ /___ /___

Description	Amount
Total	

Tuesday   Date ___ /___ /___

Description	Amount
Total	

Wednesday   Date ___ /___ /___

Description	Amount
Total	

Thursday   Date ___ /___ /___

Description	Amount
Total	

Budget: _____

Brought Forward: _____

Weekly Expense Tracker

Friday Date ___ /___ /___

Description	Amount
Total	

Saturday Date ___ /___ /___

Description	Amount
Total	

Sunday Date ___ /___ /___

Description	Amount
Total	

Notes

Budget:

Brought forward:

Weekly Expense Tracker

Monday   Date ___ /___ /___

Description	Amount
Total	

Tuesday   Date ___ /___ /___

Description	Amount
Total	

Wednesday   Date ___ /___ /___

Description	Amount
Total	

Thursday   Date ___ /___ /___

Description	Amount
Total	

Budget: _____

Brought forward: _____

Weekly Expense Tracker

Friday   Date ___ / ___ / ___

Description	Amount
Total	

Saturday   Date ___ / ___ / ___

Description	Amount
Total	

Sunday   Date ___ / ___ / ___

Description	Amount
Total	

Notes

Budget:

Brought forward:

Monthly Budget

Income

Income 1	
Income 2	
Other Income	
Total Income	

Expenses

Month

Budget

Bill to be paid	Date due	Amount	Paid	Notes

Other Expenses

Other Expenses	Date	Amount	Paid	Notes
Total				

Notes:

Total Income

Total Expenses

Difference

Weekly Expense Tracker

Monday Date ___ /___ /___

Description	Amount
Total	

Tuesday Date ___ /___ /___

Description	Amount
Total	

Wednesday Date ___ /___ /___

Description	Amount
Total	

Thursday Date ___ /___ /___

Description	Amount
Total	

Budget:

Brought forward:

Weekly Expense Tracker

Friday Date ___ /___ /___

Description	Amount
Total	

Saturday Date ___ /___ /___

Description	Amount
Total	

Sunday Date ___ /___ /___

Description	Amount
Total	

Notes

Budget: _____

Brought forward: _____

Weekly Expense Tracker

Monday
Date ___ /___ /___

Description	Amount
Total	

Tuesday
Date ___ /___ /___

Description	Amount
Total	

Wednesday
Date ___ /___ /___

Description	Amount
Total	

Thursday
Date ___ /___ /___

Description	Amount
Total	

Budget:

Brought Forward:

Weekly Expense Tracker

Friday   Date ___ /___ /___

Description	Amount
Total	

Saturday   Date ___ /___ /___

Description	Amount
Total	

Sunday   Date ___ /___ /___

Description	Amount
Total	

Notes

Budget: _____   Brought Forward: _____

Weekly Expense Tracker

Monday Date ___ /___ /___

Description	Amount
Total	

Tuesday Date ___ /___ /___

Description	Amount
Total	

Wednesday Date ___ /___ /___

Description	Amount
Total	

Thursday Date ___ /___ /___

Description	Amount
Total	

Budget: _____

Brought Forward: _____

Weekly Expense Tracker

Friday Date ___ /___ /___

Description	Amount
Total	

Saturday Date ___ /___ /___

Description	Amount
Total	

Sunday Date ___ /___ /___

Description	Amount
Total	

Notes

Budget: _____

Brought forward: _____

Weekly Expense Tracker

Monday   Date ___ /___ /___

Description	Amount
Total	

Tuesday   Date ___ /___ /___

Description	Amount
Total	

Wednesday   Date ___ /___ /___

Description	Amount
Total	

Thursday   Date ___ /___ /___

Description	Amount
Total	

Budget: _____

Brought Forward: _____

Weekly Expense Tracker

Friday Date ___ /___ /___

Description	Amount
Total	

Saturday Date ___ /___ /___

Description	Amount
Total	

Sunday Date ___ /___ /___

Description	Amount
Total	

Notes

Budget:

Brought Forward:

Weekly Expense Tracker

Monday Date ___ /___ /___

Description	Amount
Total	

Tuesday Date ___ /___ /___

Description	Amount
Total	

Wednesday Date ___ /___ /___

Description	Amount
Total	

Thursday Date ___ /___ /___

Description	Amount
Total	

Budget:

Brought forward:

Weekly Expense Tracker

Friday   Date ___ /___ /___

Description	Amount
Total	

Saturday   Date ___ /___ /___

Description	Amount
Total	

Sunday   Date ___ /___ /___

Description	Amount
Total	

Notes

Budget: Brought forward:

Monthly Budget

Income

Income 1	
Income 2	
Other Income	
Total Income	

Expenses

Month

Budget

Bill to be paid	Date due	Amount	Paid	Notes

Other Expenses

Other Expenses	Date	Amount	Paid	Notes
Total				

Notes:

Total Income

Total Expenses

Difference

Weekly Expense Tracker

Monday   Date ___ /___ /___

Description	Amount
Total	

Tuesday   Date ___ /___ /___

Description	Amount
Total	

Wednesday   Date ___ /___ /___

Description	Amount
Total	

Thursday   Date ___ /___ /___

Description	Amount
Total	

Budget:

Brought forward:

Weekly Expense Tracker

Friday   Date ___ /___ /___

Description	Amount
Total	

Saturday   Date ___ /___ /___

Description	Amount
Total	

Sunday   Date ___ /___ /___

Description	Amount
Total	

Notes

Budget:

Brought forward:

Weekly Expense Tracker

Monday
Date ___ /___ /___

Description	Amount
Total	

Tuesday
Date ___ /___ /___

Description	Amount
Total	

Wednesday
Date ___ /___ /___

Description	Amount
Total	

Thursday
Date ___ /___ /___

Description	Amount
Total	

Budget:

Brought Forward:

Weekly Expense Tracker

Friday
Date ___ /___ /___

Description	Amount
Total	

Saturday
Date ___ /___ /___

Description	Amount
Total	

Sunday
Date ___ /___ /___

Description	Amount
Total	

Notes

Budget:

Brought forward:

Weekly Expense Tracker

Monday Date ___ /___ /___

Description	Amount
Total	

Tuesday Date ___ /___ /___

Description	Amount
Total	

Wednesday Date ___ /___ /___

Description	Amount
Total	

Thursday Date ___ /___ /___

Description	Amount
Total	

Budget:

Brought forward:

Weekly Expense Tracker

Friday
Date ___ /___ /___

Description	Amount
Total	

Saturday
Date ___ /___ /___

Description	Amount
Total	

Sunday
Date ___ /___ /___

Description	Amount
Total	

Notes

Budget:

Brought forward:

Weekly Expense Tracker

Monday Date ___ /___ /___

Description	Amount
Total	

Tuesday Date ___ /___ /___

Description	Amount
Total	

Wednesday Date ___ /___ /___

Description	Amount
Total	

Thursday Date ___ /___ /___

Description	Amount
Total	

Budget: _____

Brought forward: _____

Weekly Expense Tracker

Friday   Date ___ /___ /___

Description	Amount
Total	

Saturday   Date ___ /___ /___

Description	Amount
Total	

Sunday Date ___ /___ /___

Description	Amount
Total	

Notes

Budget: _____   Brought Forward: _____

Weekly Expense Tracker

Monday   Date ___ /___ /___

Description	Amount
Total	

Tuesday   Date ___ /___ /___

Description	Amount
Total	

Wednesday   Date ___ /___ /___

Description	Amount
Total	

Thursday   Date ___ /___ /___

Description	Amount
Total	

Budget: _____

Brought Forward: _____

Weekly Expense Tracker

Friday Date ___ / ___ / ___

Description	Amount
Total	

Saturday Date ___ / ___ / ___

Description	Amount
Total	

Sunday Date ___ / ___ / ___

Description	Amount
Total	

Notes

Budget: _____

Brought forward: _____

Monthly Budget

Income

Income 1	
Income 2	
Other Income	
Total Income	

Expenses

Month

Budget

Bill to be paid	Date due	Amount	Paid	Notes

Other Expenses

Other Expenses	Date	Amount	Paid	Notes
Total				

Total Income

Total Expenses

Difference

Notes:

Weekly Expense Tracker

Monday Date ___ /___ /___

Description	Amount
Total	

Tuesday Date ___ /___ /___

Description	Amount
Total	

Wednesday Date ___ /___ /___

Description	Amount
Total	

Thursday Date ___ /___ /___

Description	Amount
Total	

Budget:

Brought forward:

Weekly Expense Tracker

Friday   Date ___ /___ /___

Description	Amount
Total	

Saturday   Date ___ /___ /___

Description	Amount
Total	

Sunday   Date ___ /___ /___

Description	Amount
Total	

Notes

Budget: Brought Forward:

Weekly Expense Tracker

Monday   Date ___ /___ /___

Description	Amount
Total	

Tuesday   Date ___ /___ /___

Description	Amount
Total	

Wednesday   Date ___ /___ /___

Description	Amount
Total	

Thursday   Date ___ /___ /___

Description	Amount
Total	

Budget: _____

Brought forward: _____

Weekly Expense Tracker

Friday   Date ___ / ___ / ___

Description	Amount
Total	

Saturday   Date ___ / ___ / ___

Description	Amount
Total	

Sunday   Date ___ / ___ / ___

Description	Amount
Total	

Notes

Budget: _____

Brought forward: _____

Weekly Expense Tracker

Monday Date ___ /___ /___

Description	Amount
Total	

Tuesday Date ___ /___ /___

Description	Amount
Total	

Wednesday Date ___ /___ /___

Description	Amount
Total	

Thursday Date ___ /___ /___

Description	Amount
Total	

Budget:

Brought forward:

Weekly Expense Tracker

Friday Date ___ /___ /___

Description	Amount
Total	

Saturday Date ___ /___ /___

Description	Amount
Total	

Sunday Date ___ /___ /___

Description	Amount
Total	

Notes

Budget: _____

Brought forward: _____

Weekly Expense Tracker

Monday   Date ___ /___ /___

Description	Amount
Total	

Tuesday   Date ___ /___ /___

Description	Amount
Total	

Wednesday   Date ___ /___ /___

Description	Amount
Total	

Thursday   Date ___ /___ /___

Description	Amount
Total	

Budget: _____

Brought Forward: _____

Weekly Expense Tracker

Friday   Date ___ /___ /___

Description	Amount
Total	

Saturday   Date ___ /___ /___

Description	Amount
Total	

Sunday   Date ___ /___ /___

Description	Amount
Total	

Notes

Budget:

Brought Forward:

Weekly Expense Tracker

Monday
Date ___ /___ /___

Description	Amount
Total	

Tuesday
Date ___ /___ /___

Description	Amount
Total	

Wednesday
Date ___ /___ /___

Description	Amount
Total	

Thursday
Date ___ /___ /___

Description	Amount
Total	

Budget:

Brought forward:

Weekly Expense Tracker

Friday   Date ___ /___ /___

Description	Amount
Total	

Saturday   Date ___ /___ /___

Description	Amount
Total	

Sunday   Date ___ /___ /___

Description	Amount
Total	

Notes

Budget:

Brought forward:

Monthly Budget

Income

Income 1	
Income 2	
Other Income	
Total Income	

Expenses

Month

Budget

Bill to be paid	Date due	Amount	Paid	Notes

Other Expenses

Other Expenses	Date	Amount	Paid	Notes
Total				

Notes:

Total Income

Total Expenses

Difference

_____

_____

_____

_____

_____

Weekly Expense Tracker

Monday   Date ___ /___ /___

Description	Amount
Total	

Tuesday   Date ___ /___ /___

Description	Amount
Total	

Wednesday   Date ___ /___ /___

Description	Amount
Total	

Thursday   Date ___ /___ /___

Description	Amount
Total	

Budget:

Brought forward:

Weekly Expense Tracker

Friday   Date ___ /___ /___

Description	Amount
Total	

Saturday   Date ___ /___ /___

Description	Amount
Total	

Sunday   Date ___ /___ /___

Description	Amount
Total	

Notes

Budget: _____

Brought forward: _____

Weekly Expense Tracker

Monday   Date ___ /___ /___

Description	Amount
Total	

Tuesday   Date ___ /___ /___

Description	Amount
Total	

Wednesday   Date ___ /___ /___

Description	Amount
Total	

Thursday   Date ___ /___ /___

Description	Amount
Total	

Budget:

Brought Forward:

Weekly Expense Tracker

Friday Date ___ /___ /___

Description	Amount
Total	

Saturday Date ___ /___ /___

Description	Amount
Total	

Sunday Date ___ /___ /___

Description	Amount
Total	

Notes

Budget:

Brought forward:

Weekly Expense Tracker

Monday   Date ___ /___ /___

Description	Amount
Total	

Tuesday   Date ___ /___ /___

Description	Amount
Total	

Wednesday   Date ___ /___ /___

Description	Amount
Total	

Thursday   Date ___ /___ /___

Description	Amount
Total	

Budget:

Brought forward:

Weekly Expense Tracker

Friday   Date ___ /___ /___

Description	Amount
Total	

Saturday   Date ___ /___ /___

Description	Amount
Total	

Sunday   Date ___ /___ /___

Description	Amount
Total	

Notes

Budget:

Brought forward:

Weekly Expense Tracker

Monday   Date ___ /___ /___

Description	Amount
Total	

Tuesday   Date ___ /___ /___

Description	Amount
Total	

Wednesday   Date ___ /___ /___

Description	Amount
Total	

Thursday   Date ___ /___ /___

Description	Amount
Total	

Budget:

Brought Forward:

Weekly Expense Tracker

Friday   Date ___ /___ /___

Description	Amount
Total	

Saturday   Date ___ /___ /___

Description	Amount
Total	

Sunday Date ___ /___ /___

Description	Amount
Total	

Notes

Budget:

Brought forward:

Weekly Expense Tracker

Monday   Date ___ /___ /___

Description	Amount
Total	

Tuesday   Date ___ /___ /___

Description	Amount
Total	

Wednesday   Date ___ /___ /___

Description	Amount
Total	

Thursday   Date ___ /___ /___

Description	Amount
Total	

Budget: _____

Brought forward: _____

Weekly Expense Tracker

Friday   Date ___ /___ /___

Description	Amount
Total	

Saturday   Date ___ /___ /___

Description	Amount
Total	

Sunday   Date ___ /___ /___

Description	Amount
Total	

Notes

Budget:

Brought forward:

Monthly Budget
Income

Income 1	
Income 2	
Other Income	
Total Income	

Expenses

Month

Budget

Bill to be paid	Date due	Amount	Paid	Notes

Other Expenses

other Expenses	Date	Amount	Paid	Notes
Total				

Notes:

Total Income

Total Expenses

Difference

Weekly Expense Tracker

Monday   Date ___ /___ /___

Description	Amount
Total	

Tuesday   Date ___ /___ /___

Description	Amount
Total	

Wednesday   Date ___ /___ /___

Description	Amount
Total	

Thursday   Date ___ /___ /___

Description	Amount
Total	

Budget: _____   Brought forward: _____

Weekly Expense Tracker

Friday   Date ___ /___ /___

Description	Amount
Total	

Saturday   Date ___ /___ /___

Description	Amount
Total	

Sunday   Date ___ /___ /___

Description	Amount
Total	

Notes

Budget:

Brought forward:

Weekly Expense Tracker

Monday Date ___ /___ /___

Description	Amount
Total	

Tuesday Date ___ /___ /___

Description	Amount
Total	

Wednesday Date ___ /___ /___

Description	Amount
Total	

Thursday Date ___ /___ /___

Description	Amount
Total	

Budget: Brought forward:

Weekly Expense Tracker

Friday

Date ___ /___ /___

Description	Amount
Total	

Saturday

Date ___ /___ /___

Description	Amount
Total	

Sunday

Date ___ /___ /___

Description	Amount
Total	

Notes

Budget:

Brought forward:

Weekly Expense Tracker

Monday Date ___ /___ /___

Description	Amount
Total	

Tuesday Date ___ /___ /___

Description	Amount
Total	

Wednesday Date ___ /___ /___

Description	Amount
Total	

Thursday Date ___ /___ /___

Description	Amount
Total	

Budget:

Brought forward:

Weekly Expense Tracker

Friday Date ___ /___ /___

Description	Amount
Total	

Saturday Date ___ /___ /___

Description	Amount
Total	

Sunday Date ___ /___ /___

Description	Amount
Total	

Notes

Budget:

Brought Forward:

Weekly Expense Tracker

Monday
Date ___ /___ /___

Description	Amount
Total	

Tuesday
Date ___ /___ /___

Description	Amount
Total	

Wednesday
Date ___ /___ /___

Description	Amount
Total	

Thursday
Date ___ /___ /___

Description	Amount
Total	

Budget:

Brought Forward:

Weekly Expense Tracker

Friday
Date ___ /___ /___

Description	Amount
Total	

Saturday
Date ___ /___ /___

Description	Amount
Total	

Sunday
Date ___ /___ /___

Description	Amount
Total	

Notes

Budget:

Brought forward:

Weekly Expense Tracker

Monday   Date ___ / ___ / ___

Description	Amount
Total	

Tuesday   Date ___ / ___ / ___

Description	Amount
Total	

Wednesday   Date ___ / ___ / ___

Description	Amount
Total	

Thursday   Date ___ / ___ / ___

Description	Amount
Total	

Budget: _____

Brought forward: _____

Weekly Expense Tracker

Friday
Date ___ /___ /___

Description	Amount
Total	

Saturday
Date ___ /___ /___

Description	Amount
Total	

Sunday
Date ___ /___ /___

Description	Amount
Total	

Notes

| |
| |
| |
| |
| |
| |

Budget:

Brought forward:

Monthly Budget

Income

Expenses

Income 1	
Income 2	
Other Income	
Total Income	

Month

Budget

Bill to be paid	Date due	Amount	Paid	Notes

Other Expenses

Other Expenses	Date	Amount	Paid	Notes
Total				

Notes:

Total Income

Total Expenses

Difference

Weekly Expense Tracker

Monday   Date ___ /___ /___

Description	Amount
Total	

Tuesday   Date ___ /___ /___

Description	Amount
Total	

Wednesday   Date ___ /___ /___

Description	Amount
Total	

Thursday   Date ___ /___ /___

Description	Amount
Total	

Budget: _____   Brought Forward: _____

Weekly Expense Tracker

Friday
Date ___ /___ /___

Description	Amount
Total	

Saturday
Date ___ /___ /___

Description	Amount
Total	

Sunday
Date ___ /___ /___

Description	Amount
Total	

Notes

Budget:

Brought Forward:

Weekly Expense Tracker

Monday Date ___ /___ /___

Description	Amount
Total	

Tuesday Date ___ /___ /___

Description	Amount
Total	

Wednesday Date ___ /___ /___

Description	Amount
Total	

Thursday Date ___ /___ /___

Description	Amount
Total	

Budget: _____

Brought Forward: _____

Weekly Expense Tracker

Friday
Date ___ /___ /___

Description	Amount
Total	

Saturday
Date ___ /___ /___

Description	Amount
Total	

Sunday
Date ___ /___ /___

Description	Amount
Total	

Notes

Budget:

Brought forward:

Weekly Expense Tracker

Monday   Date ___ /___ /___

Description	Amount
Total	

Tuesday   Date ___ /___ /___

Description	Amount
Total	

Wednesday   Date ___ /___ /___

Description	Amount
Total	

Thursday   Date ___ /___ /___

Description	Amount
Total	

Budget: _____

Brought forward: _____

Weekly Expense Tracker

Friday
Date ___ /___ /___

Description	Amount
Total	

Saturday
Date ___ /___ /___

Description	Amount
Total	

Sunday
Date ___ /___ /___

Description	Amount
Total	

Notes

Budget:

Brought forward:

Weekly Expense Tracker

Monday   Date ___ /___ /___

Description	Amount
Total	

Tuesday   Date ___ /___ /___

Description	Amount
Total	

Wednesday Date ___ /___ /___

Description	Amount
Total	

Thursday Date ___ /___ /___

Description	Amount
Total	

Budget:

Brought forward:

Weekly Expense Tracker

Friday
Date ___ /___ /___

Description	Amount
Total	

Saturday
Date ___ /___ /___

Description	Amount
Total	

Sunday
Date ___ /___ /___

Description	Amount
Total	

Notes

Budget:

Brought forward:

Weekly Expense Tracker

Monday
Date ___ / ___ / ___

Description	Amount
Total	

Tuesday
Date ___ / ___ / ___

Description	Amount
Total	

Wednesday
Date ___ / ___ / ___

Description	Amount
Total	

Thursday
Date ___ / ___ / ___

Description	Amount
Total	

Budget:

Brought forward:

Weekly Expense Tracker

Friday   Date ___ /___ /___

Description	Amount
Total	

Saturday   Date ___ /___ /___

Description	Amount
Total	

Sunday   Date ___ /___ /___

Description	Amount
Total	

Notes

Budget: _____   Brought forward: _____

Monthly Budget

Income

Income 1	
Income 2	
Other Income	
Total Income	

Expenses

Month

Budget

Bill to be paid	Date due	Amount	Paid	Notes

Other Expenses

Other Expenses	Date	Amount	Paid	Notes
Total				

Notes:

Total Income

Total Expenses

Difference

_____

_____

_____

_____

Weekly Expense Tracker

Monday
Date ___ /___ /___

Description	Amount
Total	

Tuesday
Date ___ /___ /___

Description	Amount
Total	

Wednesday
Date ___ /___ /___

Description	Amount
Total	

Thursday
Date ___ /___ /___

Description	Amount
Total	

Budget:

Brought forward:

Weekly Expense Tracker

Friday Date ___ /___ /___

Description	Amount
Total	

Saturday Date ___ /___ /___

Description	Amount
Total	

Sunday Date ___ /___ /___

Description	Amount
Total	

Notes

Budget: _____

Brought forward: _____

Weekly Expense Tracker

Monday   Date ___ /___ /___

Description	Amount
Total	

Tuesday   Date ___ /___ /___

Description	Amount
Total	

Wednesday   Date ___ /___ /___

Description	Amount
Total	

Thursday   Date ___ /___ /___

Description	Amount
Total	

Budget:

Brought forward:

Weekly Expense Tracker

Friday
Date ___ /___ /___

Description	Amount
Total	

Saturday
Date ___ /___ /___

Description	Amount
Total	

Sunday
Date ___ /___ /___

Description	Amount
Total	

Notes

Budget:

Brought forward:

Weekly Expense Tracker

Monday   Date ___ /___ /___

Description	Amount
Total	

Tuesday   Date ___ /___ /___

Description	Amount
Total	

Wednesday   Date ___ /___ /___

Description	Amount
Total	

Thursday   Date ___ /___ /___

Description	Amount
Total	

Budget:

Brought forward:

Weekly Expense Tracker

Friday Date ___ /___ /___

Description	Amount
Total	

Saturday Date ___ /___ /___

Description	Amount
Total	

Sunday Date ___ /___ /___

Description	Amount
Total	

Notes

Budget:

Brought forward:

Weekly Expense Tracker

Monday
Date ___ /___ /___

Description	Amount
Total	

Tuesday
Date ___ /___ /___

Description	Amount
Total	

Wednesday
Date ___ /___ /___

Description	Amount
Total	

Thursday
Date ___ /___ /___

Description	Amount
Total	

Budget:

Brought Forward:

Weekly Expense Tracker

Friday
Date ___ /___ /___

Description	Amount
Total	

Saturday
Date ___ /___ /___

Description	Amount
Total	

Sunday
Date ___ /___ /___

Description	Amount
Total	

Notes

Budget:

Brought forward:

Weekly Expense Tracker

Monday   Date ___ / ___ / ___

Description	Amount
Total	

Tuesday   Date ___ / ___ / ___

Description	Amount
Total	

Wednesday   Date ___ / ___ / ___

Description	Amount
Total	

Thursday   Date ___ / ___ / ___

Description	Amount
Total	

Budget:

Brought forward:

Weekly Expense Tracker

Friday Date ___ /___ /___

Description	Amount
Total	

Saturday Date ___ /___ /___

Description	Amount
Total	

Sunday Date ___ /___ /___

Description	Amount
Total	

Notes

Budget:

Brought Forward:

Monthly Budget

Income

Income 1	
Income 2	
Other Income	
Total Income	

Expenses

Month

Budget

Bill to be paid	Date due	Amount	Paid	Notes

Other Expenses

Other Expenses	Date	Amount	Paid	Notes
Total				

Notes:

Total Income

Total Expenses

Difference

Weekly Expense Tracker

Monday Date ___ /___ /___

Description	Amount
Total	

Tuesday Date ___ /___ /___

Description	Amount
Total	

Wednesday Date ___ /___ /___

Description	Amount
Total	

Thursday Date ___ /___ /___

Description	Amount
Total	

Budget:

Brought forward:

Weekly Expense Tracker

Friday
Date ___ /___ /___

Description	Amount
Total	

Saturday
Date ___ /___ /___

Description	Amount
Total	

Sunday
Date ___ /___ /___

Description	Amount
Total	

Notes

Budget:

Brought forward:

Weekly Expense Tracker

Monday   Date ___ /___ /___

Description	Amount
Total	

Tuesday   Date ___ /___ /___

Description	Amount
Total	

Wednesday   Date ___ /___ /___

Description	Amount
Total	

Thursday   Date ___ /___ /___

Description	Amount
Total	

Budget:

Brought forward:

Weekly Expense Tracker

Friday
Date ___ /___ /___

Description	Amount
Total	

Saturday
Date ___ /___ /___

Description	Amount
Total	

Sunday
Date ___ /___ /___

Description	Amount
Total	

Notes

Budget:

Brought forward:

Weekly Expense Tracker

Monday
Date ___ /___ /___

Description	Amount
Total	

Tuesday
Date ___ /___ /___

Description	Amount
Total	

Wednesday
Date ___ /___ /___

Description	Amount
Total	

Thursday
Date ___ /___ /___

Description	Amount
Total	

Budget:

Brought forward:

Weekly Expense Tracker

Friday   Date ___ /___ /___

Description	Amount
Total	

Saturday   Date ___ /___ /___

Description	Amount
Total	

Sunday   Date ___ /___ /___

Description	Amount
Total	

Notes

Brought forward:

Weekly Expense Tracker

Monday Date ___ /___ /___

Description	Amount
Total	

Tuesday Date ___ /___ /___

Description	Amount
Total	

Wednesday Date ___ /___ /___

Description	Amount
Total	

Thursday Date ___ /___ /___

Description	Amount
T	

Budget:

Brought Forward:

Budget:

Weekly Expense Tracker

Friday
Date ___ /___ /___

Description	Amount
Total	

Saturday
Date ___ /___ /___

Description	Amount
Total	

Sunday
Date ___ /___ /___

Description	Amount
Total	

Notes

Budget:

Brought Forward:

Weekly Expense Tracker

Monday   Date ___ /___ /___

Description	Amount
Total	

Tuesday   Date ___ /___ /___

Description	Amount
Total	

Wednesday   Date ___ /___ /___

Description	Amount
Total	

Thursday   Date ___ /___ /___

Description	Amount
Total	

Budget:

Brought forward:

Weekly Expense Tracker

Friday
Date ___ /___ /___

Description	Amount
Total	

Saturday
Date ___ /___ /___

Description	Amount
Total	

Sunday
Date ___ /___ /___

Description	Amount
Total	

Notes

Budget:

Brought Forward:

Notes